Becoming an OLYMPIC GYMNAST

CONTENTS

Written by Beth Tweddle

Collins

PROLOGUE

It was April 2002 and I was at the European Gymnastics Championships in Patras, Greece. I remember thinking that I didn't deserve to be there. I was up first, so I did my routine, hoping I'd do well, but not really daring to dream I'd get a European medal. No other British girl had ever won any kind of medal like that. Once I'd finished I felt happy with my performance, but all around me were the eastern European **figureheads** of gymnastics, and there I was, this little British girl shoved in the mix!

Then my competitors started going up – all these people I admired – and they started falling. So I was sitting there and my name was still in the top three on the scoreboard. Finally, the last girl went up – and she fell. Her scores came up and her name was below mine. I'd finished in third place. I'd won the bronze medal.

The moment the result appeared on the board, that was it: people started crying. My coach was in tears, my parents were in tears, the whole British **delegation** was in tears!

Suddenly I'd got a European medal, and everything had changed. My own belief changed, and I realised that I could be up there with the top gymnasts in the world. I even had a chance of going to the Olympics.

It hadn't been an easy path, though, and it didn't get any easier.

training hard

FINDING GYMNASTICS

I was walking from the age of ten months and was a nightmare around the house – always covered in bumps and bruises – and I had to be on **reins** whenever we went out anywhere. I was always under my parents' feet, always outside, always getting into mischief somehow.

My family was very hockey **orientated**, so I grew up with a hockey stick in my hand but I really wasn't interested in that, unlike my brother who played for the England youth team. I tried swimming, I tried horse-riding, I tried ballet, and eventually when I was seven I found gymnastics.

For me, being able to throw myself around and turn myself upside down in a safe environment was brilliant – plus it's not something that everyone can do. There was no decision – gymnastics was the sport that I wanted to do and that was it, so I gave up the other activities to concentrate on that.

my first taste of gymnastics, in the garden when I was seven years old

Once I'd found gymnastics, the next step was to join a club, but that's when things got a bit difficult. The thought of being left by myself really scared me. I'd always had my parents there – at hockey club and at swimming class they were always watching – but when I went to the gym they just dropped me off and that was it. So I don't know whether it was the new routine that made me nervous, but at the beginning I'd do anything not to go.

My parents realised quite soon, though, that once they got me into the gym they couldn't get me back out again – it was getting me there that was the problem. So they continued to take me, and pretty quickly I got used to the set-up and to being left on my own.

The club was in Crewe, about half an hour's drive from where we lived in Bunbury, near Chester. I'd lived there since I was one, and that's where most of my childhood was spent. It was a great village to live in – it had a very strong sense of community. Most of my early memories centre around the cricket club that my dad set up, and all my friends lived there.

with Dad's cricket club in Bunbury

In fact I basically did everything within Bunbury until about Year Four when I moved to Merton House School in Chester.

When I joined the gymnastics club I started off in the recreational class, going once a week on a Saturday morning for an hour or two. I had a natural talent. I think I was just fearless, happy to get up and have a go at things, and the coaches spotted that early on. Within a couple of months I was picked out and put through to the next level where all the **elite** girls trained.

Moving class made me nervous about going to the club all over again, and I used to get really upset. But again, as soon as I got into the gym with the other girls I trained with, I was absolutely fine.

My favourite piece of **apparatus** was always the bars: a high bar and a low bar, about 180 centimetres apart. That's what I've always been best at. I'm happy to swing around like a monkey – I have no fear of it, whereas a lot of gymnasts find the bars the hardest. As well as the bars there are three other main pieces of apparatus. There's the vault – a 25-metre run with a vaulting table at the end, which you catapult yourself over. Then there's the beam, which is ten centimetres wide: you're expected to do flicks and somersaults on it. I think that's the most nerve-wracking piece of apparatus for any gymnast during competitions. Then there's the floor: a sprung mat on which you do a prepared routine – flicks, somersaults, spins and leaps – to your own music. I think the floor is the best one to watch because the audience can feel a bit more involved in it.

In my group there were probably eight to ten of us and we were all the same age, but there were other groups of older girls training in the same room.

So, for example, we'd be on the bars, another group would be on the beam, and another group would be on the vault – there were about 30 to 40 kids in the gym at the same time.

COMPETITION TIME

Every child who wants to follow the elite path competes to get their grades, doing a different grade each year. At my first grade competition there were about 90 kids doing exactly the same routine. You have to get a certain score to be able to move on to the next grade, the next year. My first competition was for grade seven. I got a distinction and just missed out on going to the British finals, but I didn't really understand what that meant at the time. I just remember enjoying it. I thought it was quite cool, being able to perform in front of people.

in my gymnastics outfit when I was ten years old

Apparently I was a totally different child when I was in the competition environment. I was usually very nervous, and I wouldn't really speak to anyone unless I was spoken to – I'd keep myself to myself. But in a competition, I was a right little show off!

When you're young the competitions are generally early in the morning or in the afternoon, but when you get to the World Championships, they can be as late as eight o'clock at night, so you've got the whole day to occupy yourself and there's a lot of waiting – watching DVDs, listening to your MP3 player, playing computer games, doing whatever you can to try to take your mind off it. Sometimes if the competition's really late, we'll train in the morning, have lunch, then have **physio** in the afternoon and compete at night. But if it's at one or two o'clock in the afternoon you can't train in the morning because you won't have time to get back and recover.

killing time before a competition

Once you've done your routine there's not a lot you can do about the score, so I've always been less nervous waiting for the score than waiting to go on. But for me, the nerves are mixed with excitement. My coach says I'm like a dog on a leash before a competition – I'm desperate to be let off so I can show everyone what I can do.

Waiting to be let off my leash – and compete!

When you do finally go on, you do one routine on each of the four apparatus – vault, floor, bars and beam – and you get a score for each piece. Then they add all of your scores together to give you an all-around total. How well you score on each apparatus determines whether you qualify for the finals in that individual apparatus. So for instance, if you score one of the top eight scores on the bars you'll get through to the bars final. How high your all-around total is determines whether you qualify for what's called the all-around final, which means you continue on all four pieces of apparatus.

on the vault

a floor routine

a beam routine

on the bars

15

You get the start list before the competition and it says which apparatus you'll start on, and which you'll do after that – for instance, you could go from beam to floor to vault to bars. I always seem to end up starting on the beam, which is the worst one, because for me it's the hardest. I prefer to start with the vault or the bars – I don't really mind as long as the beam is in the middle!

starting on the beam

finishing on the floor

After you've done each routine you have to wait for all
the other girls to finish their routines around the competition
arena. Then as a group you move to the next piece of
apparatus. But you get your scores as you go, so you know
how well you're doing. The whole process is quite long
and a competition can take a couple of hours.

I try not to watch the other girls during a competition,
though usually the crowd gives away how well they're doing.
If I've finished a competition then I'll watch, but not before.

From a young age, we're taught not to look at the scores;
once the piece is over it's done with. If it's gone well, then
good, but if it's gone badly then there's not a lot you can do
about it, except go to the next apparatus and try not to let
your concentration slip. It can be hard, but you learn how to
cope with it from a young age. To be honest you generally
know in yourself whether you've done well or not. You can
usually tell as soon as you land whether it's been a good
or bad routine. Even now I don't think much about results
– I just move on to the next competition. When I **retire**
I'll reflect a lot more on my results, but for now I don't let
myself dwell on what I've already done. I move on and work
towards the next challenge.

landing, after a bars routine

ALL CHANGE

By the time I was ten or 11, I'd made it to the top group in my gymnastics club, but my results had started to drop. When I came 35th in a British Championship my coach explained that he'd done all he could for me and that I should probably move gyms. My parents suggested I try Liverpool, but I really didn't want to leave my friends at the club in Crewe. So one Saturday morning, instead of taking me to Crewe they took me to Liverpool without talking about it with me – and I loved it. That's when everything began to get serious. It was a bigger, high-performance club.

The coach, Amanda Reddin, was the National Senior Coach. She competed in the Olympics herself, went to the World Championships with the senior girls' team and she was just the coach to be with. I'm still with her now.

me and Amanda back when I first joined the Liverpool club

Amanda's like my second mum. I spend as much time, if not more, with her as I do with my parents. She knows me inside out. If I'm upset she can pick it up straight away. If I'm too giddy she knows exactly how to calm me down and put me in my place. She's a friend for life now. We've been through

Amanda and me celebrating in 2006

highs and lows together. She does the same amount of hours as me – whenever I'm in the gym she's there with me. She gives me my programme, and she's constantly telling me about technique problems or what's good or bad. Sometimes I need a bit of motivation, so if I'm struggling she'll encourage me. She has lots of different styles of coaching for my different moods and it just seems to work.

Moving gyms was like moving school. I'd actually just moved from my junior school to my high school, I'd just made all my new friends there and then suddenly I was having to do exactly the same switch but on the gymnastics side. I'd gone from being the big fish in a little pond to suddenly being this tiny little gymnast in a massively successful club, where I was around girls who'd been to the European and World Championships. No one at my old club had ever done that sort of thing.

It was a lot stricter at the new club. We didn't necessarily train more hours, but when we were in the gym we worked harder. In my old gym we'd have a laugh and a joke, we'd have a go and then we'd have a five-minute break, but in this club we kept going and going and going.

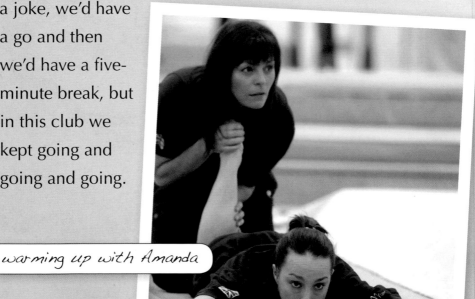

warming up with Amanda

A year and a half after I moved clubs I did the British Championships again and this time I came second, which was a pretty big leap from 35th! A lot of the coaches around the country were surprised because they'd seen my results drop and they'd thought that was it for me, so it was really nice to be back, and to see all our hard work pay off.

It was at this time, after qualifying for all four finals – bars, beam, floor and vault – at another British Championships, that I got my first real injury. I was warming up for the floor final when I landed awkwardly and broke my ankle in quite a bad place. The doctor actually told my parents and my coach that he didn't think I'd ever compete again – that that was it. I was about 13. I remember crying, not because my foot was hurting, but because I was out of the competition.

I had to have an operation, but less than a week later I was back in the gym, in a cast. At first I just did body work, strength work and flexibility. But once the pain from the operation had worn off I was back swinging around the bars again. Sometimes my coach had to support me. Sometimes I was training over soft pits so I could fall on my back without hurting my leg.

The hardest part for me was seeing a lot of the girls I trained with, who I knew were at the same sort of level as me, getting picked for their first international competitions and all I could do was sit there with a cast on, not able to do anything. I was in the cast for about ten weeks, and my real **rehabilitation** programme, to get me back to where I'd been before the injury, couldn't start until that was off. It was eight months before I could compete again.

being carried by my dad after I'd had the operation

BOUNCING BACK

A lot of people suggested I give up but I'm very stubborn; I don't like to give up. Over my career I've fought back from injury and disappointments lots of times. I like to be able to prove people wrong.

When I finally got to compete again, there was no pressure on me. Amanda just told me to go out and enjoy it – that no one was expecting anything of me because I hadn't been around for a full competition season. So I did, and it obviously worked because I came second! I was so pleased; it felt like a really important result because it came from solid hard work. Amanda had spent a lot of hours with me, telling me I could do it and to believe in myself. To come back from injury like that really proved I could do it. But up until this point I'd still never actually won anything as a Junior. I was always second or third.

Everyone kept telling me that my time would come, but I didn't really believe them. Then, when I was 16, I competed in my first Senior British competition and I won. It was the best feeling, not only because it was my first win, but also because it was a Senior competition win and I'd beaten girls two or three years older than me. Senior competitions are the ones you want to be at, that's when you can go to World Championships and the Olympic Games. You have to wait until you're in the Seniors to do any of that and I'd gone there and won. I'd finally kept my head together in a competition and suddenly my career seemed to take off.

Feeling very proud, next to my very proud coach!

GOING UP IN THE WORLD

In 2002 I went to the European Championships in Greece and won my first European medal – and that's when I really realised I could push myself even further, perhaps all the way to the Olympics?

But my next challenge was the 2002 World Championships in Hungary. They were a massive step up from the British Championships. Suddenly you're training and competing against people you aspire to be like. I loved being in that environment and really wanted to show them what I could do. I qualified for the final and again my coach just told me to go out and do what I could – no pressure.

My mum and dad go to pretty much every competition. When I was younger, this sometimes clashed with my brother's hockey matches, so my dad would go with him and Mum would come with me, but I think they've probably only missed six or seven competitions in my whole career.

So they came to Hungary to watch, but I had nothing to do with them while we were there. Once you're with the team, you're with the team, and anyway my parents know not to speak to me until after a competition. It's not that they're not allowed to, they are – everyone's got their own phone – but to be honest, my parents know that if they do phone me, I won't be very talkative before a competition. Mum always sends me a good luck text, but unless I contact them they pretty much stay away.

I didn't think I'd come in the top three, so to come fourth in that environment, at that type of competition was amazing. I was over the moon. Even though I hadn't got a medal, it was a massive achievement for British gymnastics and for me personally.

at a competition with my mum and dad – my biggest supporters

It was a busy year because I also had the Commonwealth Games in Manchester. That event was one of the highlights of my career – it was as close as I'm going to get to competing in my home town, and a lot of my school friends were able to come and watch me compete. I won, and it was amazing to have my friends and family there to celebrate with, because normally it's just my mum and dad who are there.

The day after the competition the team went shopping and people kept coming up and congratulating us. I'd never been in an environment where everyone recognised me, and it made the whole thing really **surreal**.

with my medal after the Commonwealth Games

It's the same training process for every major championship. Some athletes have different training regimes for different competitions, but for gymnastics you've just got to have the routine ready, so it's basically a question of doing it over and over again until it's perfected. It can get a bit **tedious**, but that's what you have to do.

The thing that's hard for gymnasts is that if you take three months out from training your height changes, your technique changes, your timing changes. If you're half a second out in gymnastics that's when it all goes wrong, and I've found that out many a time! If you let go of the bars too early or too late – it can be a fraction of a second – you're on your face. It's milliseconds that make the difference.

Sometimes you land and think, I wish I'd done this or that differently. But as soon as you put your arm up in front of the judge to show you're ready to start, you never know what's going to happen. I think that's the beauty of gymnastics. Someone might be winning by a mark or two, which seems like a massive lead, and then if they fall, that's them out.

just getting to the bar in time

Our training regime starts with strength work: press-ups, sit-ups, that sort of thing. We don't all necessarily have the same strength work – my coach will design a programme especially for me and whoever I'm training with.

After about three hours we have a break, then another three-hour session after lunch.

using weights to develop my arm strength

Stretching increases my flexibility.

sit-ups to work my stomach muscles

35

UNDER PRESSURE

At this time in my career, after the 2002 Commonwealth Games, it felt like every time I went to a competition I was getting another result that was making history. I think my self-belief was changing and I wanted more of those records. I constantly wanted to be better than my last result.

As I competed at a higher and higher level I put more and more pressure on myself. I'd done all the hard work in the gym, so I wanted to achieve the best result I could. Most of the time the pressure that's on me is actually from myself. My coach only ever tells me to do what I do in the gym, never what to score or what place to finish in.

37

SCHOOL COMES FIRST

Despite doing very well at my gymnastics, school was very much the main focus up until my GCSEs, which was fine with me because I'd always loved school, mainly because I liked being around my friends. I wasn't necessarily as keen on all the work!

At primary school I found Maths and Science easy but I really struggled with English. I wasn't the biggest fan of reading when I was a kid, but now, when I go away I always have a book with me. I think the problem was that I was too **hyperactive**; I didn't like sitting still. I wasn't a child who would be in one place for more than an hour, so to sit down and concentrate on reading a book was something that I found really hard. Also, with Maths there's always a correct answer and because I'm quite a **perfectionist** that suited me: add two and two and you get an answer. You have to be a lot more creative and imaginative to write a story – there isn't a set thing to write, you have to think about it.

in my school uniform

By the time I got to senior school, I was an international gymnast so my parents had to explain to my teachers that I might need a week off here and there, that I might need time off to do training camps, and that sometimes the work might get too much for me. But even then my parents always insisted that I focus on my school work. I was never allowed a day off if I was tired after a competition, and I always had to get my homework done.

By the lower end of senior school, I was training five days a week, doing about 25 hours, which is quite a lot, but to me it was just what I did. I used to get up and go to school in the morning, train after school, get home at about ten at night, have my tea, do my homework, go to bed and then start it all over again.

A-Levels were a bit different. That's when my foot came off the pedal with school. I started off doing three A-Levels: Maths, Physics and Biology. During the first two months of my sixth form, I was away competing at the World Championships, so all my work was sent to me and I had to do it and send it back. I started to struggle with Maths, so I decided to drop it and just do Physics and Biology, and I passed both of them.

Trying to constantly juggle school work with gymnastics was hard enough and didn't leave much time for anything else, certainly not a social life, but my mum and dad were very supportive of me seeing my friends when I could. So, on a Saturday afternoon when I'd finished training, if there was a party or people were arranging to go in to town, they'd drop me off on the way home. Although they were strict about me getting my school work done, they also made sure that I still had a good set of friends around me and I didn't separate myself off too much. Sometimes, on a Monday morning when I went in to school and everyone was talking about the parties they'd been to and what the gossip was, I felt a bit left out because I'd been in the gym. But I was lucky that I had a really good group of friends; they collected school work for me, and they understood that my training was important to me.

If they asked me to go to a party and I said no, they didn't take it as me not wanting to be their friend. They took it for what it was – that I needed to train.

When I started going to international competitions my friends were always interested in where I was going, so I used to take in my Great Britain tracksuits and the videos to show them what I'd been doing. As my career became more and more high profile and I started being in the local papers, my friends knew I wasn't just skiving off school here, there and everywhere and they were really supportive. When I look back I don't feel like I've missed much. I've gained a lot more than I lost out on.

being interviewed for the television

When I finished school I spent a whole year training solidly with no distractions – no studying – and apparently I was a nightmare! I'd always been a very busy person and so as soon as all I had was gymnastics, I found it really hard to switch off. I didn't enjoy my training as much, so my coach was actually quite **adamant** that she wanted me to do something else as well as gymnastics.

I was lucky because Liverpool John Moores University approached me and suggested I apply for a sports **scholarship**, and agreed to take me with my two A-levels.

My coach was very supportive of me going to university. She worked my training timetable around my university timetable. I don't know how I did it, but having both things on the go meant that I could switch off from university and go to the gym, or if I was struggling in the gym I could switch off and go and see all my university friends. Rather than being too much, I found the two parts of my life **complemented** each other perfectly.

My training was number one, my university work was number two and my social life was number three.

Training became fun again when it wasn't all I did.

Competitions and exams often clashed, so I had to stay focused to succeed at both.

had a mentor at university, if I missed work they'd send it or email it to me and they'd arrange extra time with tutors if I was struggling with work – they helped me as much as they could. But it was pretty full-on, often with exams and competitions clashing, and I actually did my final exams the day after a European final.

I think because my family was very orientated towards going to university – my brother went, my cousins went – I just thought that was the usual pathway. I didn't want to be any different so I never really considered not going. You went to school, you went to high school, you did your A-Levels and then you went to university. I just had to combine that path with the gymnastic one. I also knew that without an education, if something happened – if I got injured and couldn't carry on with gymnastics – I wouldn't have anything to fall back on, so it was important in that sense too.

graduating from university – another proud day for the Tweddle family

The 2004 Athens Olympics took place in the same year
I started my university course. The actual competition
at the Olympics is pretty much the same as the World
Championships, but everything else surrounding the
Olympics is totally different. I only found out three or
four weeks before we flew to the holding camp that I was
actually part of the 2004 Olympic team. Suddenly I got
all these letters from people congratulating me and then,
before I knew it, I was off!

I remember going to Earls Court to pick up the kit the day after I'd been selected, and I couldn't believe it. I was buzzing – so excited. My brother was very jealous when I came home with it which made it even more fun!

We stayed in the holding camp in Barcelona for two weeks before flying to Athens and moving into the Olympic Village for the next two and a half weeks.

the Athens Olympic Village

The Olympic Village is like a little community, but you can be walking down the street and you'll see athletes like Usain Bolt or Michael Phelps! It's a totally different world. There are so many distractions: arcades, 24-hour food halls, internet access, discos at night – anything that you want to do is there, but our coaches were quite strict with us before the competition, and they kept us away from all that.

The team all stayed in one flat, and I shared a room with another gymnast, Lizzie Line. I took all my cards and pictures with me to put up around the room. Between us, my flatmate and I tried to make it homely. Tim Henman, the tennis player, was in the flat opposite, and we were all very excited because he was a massive name. It's kind of weird to be in a position where you're suddenly socialising with all these famous people.

Lizzie and me

Up until the competition everything was quite strict and structured in terms of what we could do, the training programme and what we could eat. We didn't have a specific diet but over the years I've learnt how to control my body weight and I know what's best for me during training and competitions. I have cereal or toast for breakfast, then my main meal at lunchtime – something like chicken, rice, pasta, lasagne – and then a smaller meal in the evening – salad, soup, something plain like that. Once the competition was over though, we were allowed to do what we wanted, eat what we wanted and go and experience the Olympics.

I was really interested in the hockey matches at the Olympics, as my brother plays the sport, too.

The team came 11th and I qualified for the all-around final. So everyone else had finished but I had to carry on training, and then two days later I had to compete again. I was very upset not to have qualified for the bars final, which I only just missed out on, and I think that disappointment might have affected my performance in the all-around final, so I didn't do quite as well as I'd hoped. I had a nightmare on the beam, which was my first piece: I think I fell twice, so it messed up my finishing place, which was down in 19th, when I'd been hoping to be in the top 15. Every other piece was fine – in fact the other three pieces went really well.

I think that because I knew I'd already messed up the beam I relaxed – it took the pressure off because it didn't matter any more, so I could just go for it. My coach was pleased with me in that sense because I hadn't let my head totally drop and messed up the rest of the competition, but obviously she was disappointed with my beam performance.

at the bars final, Athens

My mum, dad and brother had all come out, which was really nice, and as soon as the competition was over I was able to spend lots of time with them. We went to other Olympic events, like swimming, diving and athletics, and really made the most of being there.

diving finals in Athens

Kelly Holmes winning the final of the Women's 1,500 metre race in Athens

INJURY TIME

After the Olympics, I was operated on to take little loose bone fragments out of my feet. It's just wear and tear that happens over the years. We made the decision to do both feet at once, to avoid having to put me under anaesthetic twice. For the first 48 hours after the operation I was on a skateboard, wheeling myself around the house! After only a couple of days I was walking fine and two weeks later I was back bouncing about.

Then in 2005 I went to the European Championships in Hungary. I was in the middle of the all-around final when I came off the bars, landed on my back and hit my head on the floor. Apparently I got up straight away and crawled to the side but when my doctor came to check on me I was in my own little world. I didn't have a clue what was going on. I was stretchered out – spinal board and everything – and taken off to hospital. I remember waking up in the ambulance and thinking I needed to warm up for the beam. The next thing I knew I was in the X-ray room, with all these doctors speaking Hungarian around me.

on the spinal board, in a neck collar, terrified

Waking up on a spinal board with a collar around my neck was one of the scariest moments of my career. I didn't know where I was or why I was there – it was horrible.

They organised for me to have a **CT scan** and it was all clear, so they let me leave the hospital, but my doctor had to stay in my room that night and wake me up every hour to check that I was still doing all right. Luckily it was just **concussion** and by the next day I felt I could have competed, but my doctor said that I wasn't allowed to because I couldn't remember what had happened. All I could do was sit and watch everyone else, but two weeks later I was back in the UK and competing again. In that sense it didn't actually affect my career that much.

The next year, 2006, started off pretty badly too. I went to Melbourne for the Commonwealth Games and was injured again, so I had to support the team from the sidelines as they won a silver medal. Everyone thought I'd be fit again in three weeks, but it took much longer than that in the end.

I really wanted to compete in the European Championships a month later. Finally our doctor, who's put me back together so many times before, gave me the all-clear to fly out to compete only two days before we were due to leave.

on my crutches with Dan Keatings, who was also injured in the Commonwealth Games

I qualified for the bars final, and won it. That was my first ever European title and it put a smile back on my face after a pretty rough couple of months.

Then 2006 just got better and better when I won the World title.

The World Championships were held in Denmark that year. I did my routine on the bars, landing the dismount perfectly, and I just knew that it was the best I could have done. I remember waiting for my score, but after that it's all a bit of a blur. I remember being given a flag and running around the arena with it. That was the first time I'd really seen my coach over the moon – she just didn't know what to do with herself. My mum and dad were crying and didn't know what to do with themselves either! To hear the national anthem on a world stage and know that I was the first ever British gymnast to win a World title was a massive thing for everyone.

I went to all the press conferences and then went back to the hotel and had a huge party with the team. It was a night I won't forget.

I had the floor final the next day but I didn't go to bed until about three in the morning, and when I did I couldn't sleep because I was so excited. All night I was doing the bars routine over and over in my head, thinking about what could have gone wrong, but it hadn't – everything had just gone perfectly. Then my alarm went off and I got straight out of bed, ready for the next day's competition – I wasn't tired in the slightest.

I did the floor final and it was the easiest floor routine I've ever done because I was on cloud nine. My coach started crying before I even began my routine because when I walked out onto the floor, I was announced as "Beth Tweddle, World Champion". It was the best feeling in the world.

over the moon and in total shock

That whole week I was doing lots of interviews and everyone was saying that I'd be **nominated** for Sports Personality of the Year, but I didn't really believe them. I was already scheduled to perform at the event, which was nerve-wracking enough because they'd set the bars up in the middle of the room when normally you've got lots of space around them. So, there were all these famous athletes sitting around where I had to perform, and I kept thinking that if I went too far sideways I'd end up on the footballer Alan Shearer's lap!

finishing my routine at the Sports Personality of the Year awards

with Gary Lineker, Zara Phillips, Darren Clarke and Sue Barker at the awards ceremony

I came third in the Sports Personality of the Year, which I was amazed about because gymnastics has never been a high-profile sport: no gymnast had ever even been in **contention** before. It meant a lot to me. Gymnastics is what I do and what I aim towards, but suddenly it felt like the public recognised and appreciated all the hard work I'd put into it, and they liked what I'd done.

THE 2008 BEIJING OLYMPICS

In 2008 I went to my second Olympics, in Beijing. In some ways the experience was pretty much the same as Athens. You get the kit, you get to stay in the flat. Unfortunately I only did two apparatus – bars and floor. I got an internal rib injury the day we flew out to our holding camp in Hong Kong. At first we didn't think anything of it, then when we got there I was really struggling, to the stage where it was keeping me up at night. So they scanned me and found that I had an internal bleed. It was only small, but it was the most painful thing ever: I couldn't cough, couldn't laugh.

So I was pulled out of training. All I was allowed to do was a bit of swimming, which obviously leading up to an Olympics is not the best preparation.

The rest of the team flew out to Beijing and left me behind in the holding camp trying to get fit.

It was hard, but my coach stayed behind with me and we made every effort. Normally I'd only train twice a day but now I was training three times a day to get fit. I was desperate to compete. When I first found out about the injury I'd thought that was it, my Olympics was over, but eventually I flew out to Beijing and competed with the rest of the team.

training hard, determined to compete

the Beijing Olympic Village

63

The team came ninth, which was brilliant, and we only just missed out on team finals. Then I qualified for the bars final, but finished fourth, which was the most disappointing result of my career. I was so close to third place, to a medal and to all my dreams, but at the same time so far from it all. It was devastating.

the bars final - so close to a medal

Afterwards I kept reliving and reliving the routine, and my phone was going constantly with people wanting to talk to me. I just wanted to turn my attention away from the whole Olympics. I didn't want anything to do with it. We came home, but the Olympics were all over the TV, so I went to a travel agent and booked myself a holiday, leaving the next day. I actually ended

on my way home – dejected and disappointed

up having a really good time. It was a bit weird because I was getting recognised a lot, but it gave me time to relax and to think. I'd thought, after Beijing, that I wouldn't compete in the next Olympics in 2012 – I couldn't think that far ahead, and wasn't sure if I could pick myself up and dedicate myself again after such a disappointment. But while I was away I was just itching to get back in the gym, and so I realised that I wasn't ready to retire.

When I came home I went straight back to the gym, but during training I noticed that my shoulder was sore and by the next day I could only just lift my arm.

We got the doctors to have a look at it and they explained that I needed another operation. I was really upset and started to question whether I could carry on. I'd not got the result I wanted in Beijing and now I needed another operation. But I think deep down I wasn't ready to give up on what I wanted. So I had the operation, got fit again in time for the European Championships, and won two titles. That's when I knew I'd carry on: because I still enjoyed the training, I still enjoyed getting the results and I was still able to get the results. It made me realise that the decision to keep going had been the right one.

ANOTHER FALL, ANOTHER VICTORY

Later on that year, the World Championships were held in London. I'd already qualified for the floor final and then I fell during the bars qualification, which was the piece that everyone was expecting me to win.

It was a nasty fall, but I wasn't hurt.

disbelief at the fall, but the crowd gave me the courage to carry on

I could hear the crowd's disappointment. I thought that was my World Championship over, but then everyone started clapping and cheering, so I got up and finished my routine and had a smile on my face as I walked off. I kept a brave face until I saw my mum and dad and then burst into tears. I just wanted to go home, I didn't want to be there, but I had to stay the whole week, training for the floor final.

There was no pressure on me for the floor final. I wasn't expected to win and all anyone was talking about was my fall, so my coach just told me to go and enjoy it. After all, I had nothing to lose. The crowd was amazing – 15,000 people shouting my name. I did my routine and knew as soon as I'd finished that it was the best I could have done.

It was nerve-wracking, because I was first up and there were eight of us in the final, so I just sat waiting for every single score to come through. It got to the stage where I was guaranteed a bronze medal, but as soon as I knew I was in the medals I wanted the gold one! Then the last girl made a slight mistake and you could see that that was it: the title was mine. It was an emotional rollercoaster of a week. I'd had the downfall with the bars and then suddenly to win a World title a week later was something I'd never dreamt would happen.

It felt different to other competitions because everyone knew me as a bars worker and not everyone knew me as a floor worker. The pressure wasn't really on to win it and I think the fact that it wasn't my specialist piece made it all the more special to me.

a very proud gold medal win

MEETING PRINCE CHARLES

In October 2009 I found out that I'd been awarded an **MBE** – but I wasn't allowed to tell anyone until the end of December. Of course I didn't want my family finding out something like that in the media so I told them at Christmas, and my nana and granny started crying. It meant so much to them, and that made me realise what a big deal it was.

I went to the palace to receive the medal from Prince Charles. It felt really formal and quite **intimidating**. You have to wait in line and are told exactly what to do – walk up, do a turn, take three steps forward and curtsy.

Prince Charles awarding me my MBE at Buckingham Palace

with my MBE

I was more nervous doing that than I was doing my routine at the Olympics! But seeing how much younger I was than most of the other people there made me feel really proud: it showed me how much I'd achieved.

There's still one thing I'd love, and that's to have an Olympic medal in my collection. I want to look back at my career and think I tried to win it, rather than retire and wish I'd tried, so that's why I'm continuing to 2012. I'm looking forward to it: it's going to be a massive event for the whole of the UK.

I'm now training about 30 hours a week, plus physio, plus ballet twice a week. The ballet is a new part of my training; it helps with my **posture** and dance. It's actually been pretty good fun – it's something different and I'm really enjoying it.

Although the demands of training are high – it takes up so much of my time that it doesn't leave much room for anything else – it's worth it when I get to a competition. Competing is still what I enjoy the most and it makes all the hard work in the gym worthwhile.

As a young kid I never dreamt of even going to the Olympics, never mind being an Olympic or World Champion, so in that sense, I've already outdone anything that I ever thought I would do in gymnastics. Anything that I do from now on is a bonus.

GLOSSARY

adamant	determined
apparatus	equipment
complemented	worked well together; completed
concussion	a minor injury to the brain caused by being hit or by striking your head
contention	competition
CT scan	a type of X-ray that uses computers to produce a 3D image of the inside of the body
delegation	people attending an event as representatives of a country or organisation
elite	very best and most gifted
figureheads	people at the very top of their sport or profession
hyperactive	unable to keep still even for short periods of time
intimidating	making you feel you're not very good at something
MBE	short for "Member of the Order of the British Empire", an award given to British citizens who have done something exceptional
nominated	put forward for an award or a position
orientated	focused on, interested in
perfectionist	someone who feels they have to do everything perfectly
physio	short for physiotherapy, a treatment that uses exercise and massage to heal the body
posture	how you stand or hold your body
rehabilitation	the process of getting better after an injury
reins	long straps attached to small children to stop them running off
retire	give up a job or a sport
scholarship	money given to someone to cover the cost of their studies
surreal	unreal in a bizarre way
tedious	boring

INDEX

2002: won Gold
at the Commonwealth
Games, Manchester

1998: came
second at the British
Championships

2001: won
first Senior British
Competition

1992: started
gymnastics

1998: injured
at the British
Championships

1994:
first grade
competition

low

1992   1994   1998   2001

78

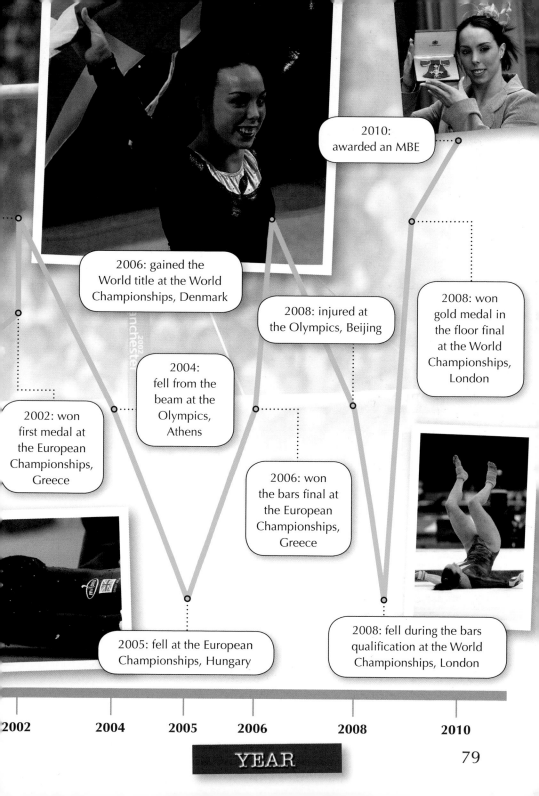

2010: awarded an MBE

2006: gained the World title at the World Championships, Denmark

2008: injured at the Olympics, Beijing

2008: won gold medal in the floor final at the World Championships, London

2004: fell from the beam at the Olympics, Athens

2002: won first medal at the European Championships, Greece

2006: won the bars final at the European Championships, Greece

2005: fell at the European Championships, Hungary

2008: fell during the bars qualification at the World Championships, London

2002   2004   2005   2006   2008   2010

YEAR

Ideas for reading

Written by Clare Dowdall, PhD
Lecturer and Primary Literacy Consultant

Reading objectives:
- draw inferences such as inferring characters' feelings, thoughts and motives from their actions, and justify inferences with evidence
- retrieve, record and present information from non-fiction
- provide reasoned justifications for their views
- summarise the main ideas drawn from more than one paragraph, identifying key details that support the main ideas
- identify how language, structure and presentation contribute to meaning

Spoken language objectives:
- participate in discussions and role play
- maintain attention and participate actively in collaborative conversations
- articulate and justify answers, arguments and opinions

Curriculum links: Citizenship; P.E.

Interest words: apparatus, contention, delegation, elite, nominated, perfectionist, physio, rehabilitation

Resources: pens, paper, voice recorder

Build a context for reading

This book can be read over two or more reading sessions.

- Look at the cover and title together. Ask children what activity Beth Tweddle is doing in the photo and if they know anything about her career as a gymnast.

- Discuss children's prior knowledge of the Olympics, who would like to go to an Olympic Games and which events would be of the most interest to the children.

- Explain that this book is an autobiography. Discuss what an autobiography is, and what the prefix *auto* means. Revise the features that are likely to be found in an autobiography, e.g. *written in chronological order and in the first person.*

Understand and apply reading strategies

- Ask children to read to p9 silently and consider how Beth's experiences from her childhood may have helped to shape her career as an adult. Remind children to look for clues for meaning in the root words and to use the glossary for emboldened words.